hedgerows

tanka pentaptychs

Joy McCall

Keibooks, Perryville, Maryland, USA, 2014

ISBN 978-0692200988 (Print)
Also available for Kindle.

Keibooks
P O Box 516
Perryville, MD 21903
http://AtlasPoetica.org
Keibooks@gmail.com

when I die
my wandering soul
will catch
on hedgerow thorns, then fall
to the dark Norfolk soil

Joy McCall

for all my kinfolk

and for my mother,
who taught me to love the hedgerows

Joy McCall

she is off
with a simple
goodbye
stepping from her bed
into more elegant shoes

Brian Zimmer

Acknowledgements

*Many of these strings have appeared in Atlas Poetica
and some in Bright Stars, Skylark, The Tanka Journal,
Ribbons, The Bamboo Hut and Poetry Nook. I thank
the editors for their generous acceptances.*

Joy McCall

Table of Contents

I throw
blood-red berries
on the fire
a dark hawthorn spike
pins my soul to the earth

underground
the sound of the waves
and the wind
a constant singing
through the soil

the North Sea
grinds the shells and bones
into sand
it devours the land
little by little

the churches
are in ruins
their graveyards
abandoned to grasses
briars and weeds

red poppies
and small grey stones
litter the fields
bones of man and beasts
fill the bedrock

stitching
it all together
the winding threads,
the tangled hedgerows:
hazel, hawthorn, brambles

Norfolk, England

Introduction

It has been two years since Canadian poet Lynda
Monahan submitted a tanka sequence co-written with Joy
McCall for publication in my journal *Atlas Poetica : A
Journal of Poetry of Place in Contemporary Tanka*. In the
wake of that acceptance, Joy was emboldened to send her
own individual submission featuring tanka about her city of
Norwich in England. She quoted Langston Hughes, "Hold
fast to dreams / for if dreams die / life is a broken-winged
bird / that cannot fly." Thus began a two year
correspondence in poetry through which I have come to
know this extraordinary soul.

To write tanka requires an eye for meaningful detail and
the ability to evoke a connection: good tanka are pebbles
thrown into the mind of the receptive reader. Joy has that
eye, and added to it, a compassionate soul that meets others
without judgment. She takes a keen interest in everything
from her children to the local crooks and drunks, artisans,
madwomen, and ghosts. The supernatural is as real to her as
the material world and the dead populate her poems along
with the living. The fleshless rabbi walking his haunted
corridor reminds her that Norwich was the origin of the
Blood Libel against the Jews, while not far away the witches
still dance among the standing stones. Old churches, old
pubs, and old graves tell stories to those that listen amid the
scattered needles and barroom fights of the present day.

Corn marks, graffiti, or poetry, humans scratch at the
bones of the world to leave a record of their existence. Joy is
no different. We all know we are mortal; we all know that we
will die. We all want to resist the great silence, so we rebel
by talking, writing, loving, and fighting. What Joy knows is
not only will she die, but that she is dying right now, dying as
she types, dying in these pages, dying nerve by nerve and
cell by cell. She is scratching her words into the fabric of her

world and her message is the same as every scribbler, vandal, and artist has left behind: *I was here.*

Human flesh is perishable, and so are human spirits. Amputated and paraplegic as a result of a motorcycle accident, Joy knows that better than most. Unlike most, she was a nurse before her accident, so she had already tended the broken bodies of others and wrapped their corpses when they died. With metal spikes sprouting from her shattered legs and a dead boy in the next bed, she understands pain and fear. Lately, as the damage extends to her brain, she fears losing her mind.

And still the poems come.

Shiki wrote while dying of tuberculosis. Takuboku wrote while working in an asylum. This is the difference between tanka of the modern world and the tanka of the classic poets of old Japan. The poet-courtiers deliberately eschewed the misery of the material world and left behind a seductive vision of a beautiful world. Joy's world is every bit as beautiful, but real and solid, even when it contains ghosts and poison and curses and despair.

At first Joy didn't send me those poems; she hadn't seen that sort of thing published in tanka and wasn't certain anyone would want them. She sent me an example:

> a back street
> in Great Yarmouth
> by the sea—
> a thin hooker screams abuse
> at sailors passing her by

I immediately offered to publish it. She asked, "You sure?" She had always written tanka like this—'hooker' is No. 895 in her journal. I told her that contemporary Japanese and Japanese American tanka poets have written about menstruation, political demonstrations, oil wells, discrimination, and farts. Everything is tanka.

I have published a great many of Joy's tanka in the venues I have edited, including *Atlas Poetica : A Journal of Poetry of Place in Contemporary Tanka* and *Bright Stars, An Organic Tanka Anthology*, as well as special features and anthologies. She then hired me to edit her first collection of tanka, *circling smoke, scattered bones*. Not an experienced editor, she sent me every tanka she'd written: 2300 of them poured into my inbox. I selected several hundred and arranged them into chapters.

Meanwhile, she collaborated with Tim Lenton, another Norwich poet, to produce *Stillness lies deep : Tanka poems from Norfolk*. She has continued to write, to write while recuperating from various medical procedures, while her mother was dying, and while workmen rebuilt the front of her house after a car plowed into it in the middle of the night. Through all this, she has been a supporter of emerging poets. She has co-written sequences with poets ranging from experienced tanka poets like Sanford Goldstein to emerging poets like Matsukaze and Eamonn O'Neill. In spite of all this, she has found the energy to produce a third book of tanka poetry.

This time, Joy has written and collected ninety-five tanka pentaptychs (short sequences of five tanka) to form *Hedgerows : Tanka Pentaptychs*. The result is an intensely personal journey through the country within and around her. However much she cavils at the limitations of her wheelchair, she manages to go places and do things those with stronger legs and weaker spirits have never tried. If you read this book, you will follow the ley lines she has blazed to find yourself in a magic land.

M. Kei
Publisher, Keibooks
29 March 2014

Joy McCall

witches

solstice night
I asked the witches
about age and death
they smiled sadly at me
and went on dancing

all those
dark ancient spirits
stalk these streets
hiding inside the faces
of passersby

worn steps
the ducking stool
on the bridge
the river below carries
women, drowning

the witches
in a dark circle
humming low
no boys to sacrifice now
still the air is heavy with death

into the henge
where the crones danced
in the darkness
comes the dawn, and cold ashes
blowing around the stones

Arminghall Henge, Norfolk

rituals

the wax melts
the room fills with the scent
of dark coffee
shadows dance on the walls
ash settles on the beams

the smallest candles
burn in sake cups
anagama
stained from the pit-fire
the smoke circling

pale sake
warming in the red cup
fire embers
these rituals calm
the echoing spaces

dark things move
in candlelight
a small creature
runs under the chair
soundless, traceless

tonight I lit
all the candles
for him
I did not ring the bells,
let him sleep in peace

The holy room

animus

I know him
the dark-skinned man
waiting there
his footprints crossing
the tide-wet sand

when I am distant
he hunches in the cave
arms round his knees
looking out to sea
missing my voice

I do not know
any of his names
though I ask
he never speaks
he takes my hand, smiling

all my life
I have walked
with this man
we are the same bones
the same dry dust

in the cave
darkness beckons
night calls
the waves below, crash
he lights the fire

Inner lands

see-saw

across the fields
the violin sings
high and sweet
the cello echoes low
a slow sad tune

ragged children
in the playground
stop, listen
the see-saw settles
and is still

the music ends
small listeners wait
there is no more
play begins again
the see-saw rocking

over the field
a song in high voices
the old rhyme
see-saw Margery Daw
Johnny shall have a new master

I write, waiting
for his gentle reply
how long?
the muse is lonely
in the silent playground

ghosts

a spirit
in the bookshop
in Tipp, Ohio
a small child humming
a settlers' hymn

on a cliff
above a Welsh cove
an old cottage
a gentle ghost
folds back the quilts

friday nights
the sound of a hammer
on an anvil
a blacksmith singing
by the old forge wall

on the cliff
a bent old woman
talking to herself
through her grey body
I see the waves breaking

in the old hall
where the strangers dwelt
a robed rabbi walks
he repeats sacred words
there is no flesh on his bones

Strangers' Hall, Norwich

names

a cold wind blows
in the walled garden
among the trees
a bearded visionary
a persian woman

a small bird sits
on her shoulder
whispering
a message from a man
she does not know

eyes are watching
my fingers touch
stone faces
I say nothing
the walls have ears

the sculptor
smells of cedar chips
and cat mint
he speaks of old poems
and unrequited love

I ask the names
of these old ones
who stand
among the herbs
he says *I do not know*

The Old Bungay Road, Norfolk

bones

must I go
to the dark grave
without knowing
the thin bones of his hand
as it holds the pen?

ancient masks
skulls and cross-bones
hang on the walls
they creep into ink
under the skin

in times past
I lay down, and sleep
came easy
now my bones ache
the bed feels like old straw

sages found
omens in dry bones
in the cracks
when my bones broke
they told only the past

dragon skin
the ancient dzi bead
tells its tale
the pattern scratched
by old bones, old teeth

the tribe

from the roots
the wild tribe comes
one by one
circling the tree, they dance
on the hill until dawn

hand in hand
these strange small people
dance and sing
their fingers white as roots
their skin rough as bark

their voices
are the creaking of trees
in the dark wind
their footsteps are dry nuts
falling on soft ground

how they smile
with teeth like the bones
of harvest mice
their hair prickles
like chestnut spikes

when they laugh
it is the stream flowing
the spring bubbling
they slip away to sleep at noon
drunk on rain

Joy McCall

sanctuary

dusty shed
the holy of holies
back then
safe hiding place
dark corners

on tiptoes
through the crack
I'd see the man
thin stick in hand
beating time

it was years
before I grew
too tall to hide
and he took me
into the old house

and dawn came . . .
and long dawns after
and I watched
from the high window
a bird, nesting on the shed

and oh
I wanted to be small then
and brown-winged
and silently safe again
and holy

martyrs

noisy
the great factory
sprawls
from the river's edge
to the railway sidings

the machines
throw off engine oil
and cutting swarf
exhaustion and despair
dirt and disease

generations
of Norfolk men
lose fingers
and hands and hope
martyrs to the machine

still they come
as their fathers did
till they are old
fighting with the steel
they lose, they die

and far away
in the colonies
in the oceans
where their engines turn
no one knows their names, or cares

Machine shop, Norwich

Joy McCall

desolation road

the girl
looked up from the gutter
and took his hand
they found her at dawn
torn in the alley

through the night
the cathedral bells
strike the hour
in its dark shadow
clubbers drink around the clock

one long street
named for the old Prince
from rural Wales
crawls now with misery
twenty-four hour drinking

white powder
in all the washrooms
on this strip
the dealer makes his fortune
on desolation road

he collects
on Saturday nights
making rounds
at Sunday Mass, a thick wad
in the collection plate

through the rushes

the kappa
at the edge of the stream
dripping water
takes a reed and writes
on the sandbank

his head tilts
water drips from the bowl
I drink
his long green fingers
stroke my arm

wind blows
through the rushes
rustling
I write words that begin
with r and s and t

on the stream
rain begins to fall
the kappa smiles
his bowl filling
he is content

from midstream
he brings me a song
and a silver fish
I let the fish go
and sit, writing tanka

trapped

For Lee

in the cell
he dreams of freedom
his spirit
gone to ground, hiding
in the long grass in the field

winter full moon
another good friend
hangs dead
the floors hide old bones
men go mad

locked in
solitary confinement
he writes
I am trapped, and he knows
paralysed, I understand

in spring
he walks through
the barred gates
into a world
he has forgotten

he stands
looking at trees
and rainclouds
and until night falls
he watches the sky, and waits

nevermore

once I had
no fear of the open road
nor of speed
now, on every corner
shadows hide dark pits

I dream
I'm walking among trees
in the dusk
the sound of one foot
dragging on the peat

even when
I say the word
paralysed
it makes no sense
still I walk, I run, I dance

how happy
my spirit would be
on its own
unencumbered
by this heavy shell

nevermore
the raven's words
the old cry
the ache to stand again
on solid ground

over the rail

the landlady
of the harbour pub
leans on the bar
and calls out
time gentlemen, please

peasants
and sour-faced villagers
down their ale
and smoking rank roll-ups
they stagger home

some sailors
already loudly drunk
call for more ale
the captain stands
swaying on his feet

a small child
in the doorway
cries *father*
the old seaman pales
lays the tankard down

back on the ship
while the sailors sleep
the captain
stares at the dark sea
weeping, calling *my son, my son*

Orford Ness, Suffolk, England

tombland

around the corner
from the all-night bars
an old church
the cobblestone path leads
to untended graves

damp and cool
and musty, inside
a woman sits
dim light filters
through grimy windows

distant thump
of music, and clubbers
shouting and singing
the woman lifts her head
her prayers disturbed

on the hard pew
she settles to sleep
shivering
rain begins to fall
rats scratch behind the altar

below the nave
thick lime in the pit
shifts a little
then closes again
over nameless small corpses

St. George's, Tombland, Norwich

all souls' night

in the dark
down the hall
Anne Boleyn
carries her head
under her arm

the black dog
haunts the flatlands
howling
children wake screaming
dark Shuck snarling at the door

midnight
and at the pub door
the hanged priest knocks
the weary landlord brings
the penitential ale

the ferry drifts
down and across the river
on the tide
night after night, plague souls
leave the doomed village

all souls' night
across the empty park
the shadows creep
and through the lonely dark
a woman weeps

brown

my yearning
for the brown of earth
never ends—
my skin, my flesh, my bones
pulled by the dark soil

a brown aching
for the land, the rocks,
the grainy sand
scratched with hawthorn spikes
my blood runs brown

the gentleness
of sanded walnut wood
in my pale hands—
one day I will disappear
into sap and bark

the quiet voices
of my homelands
are brown—
a gentle sighing
across furrowed fields

the deer
watches me
with brown eyes—
I slip through furred skin
to sleep in her warm belly

Allah

I wake
hooked to machines
I can't move
there is a dead boy
in the next bed, staring

by my bed
a dark muslim
his eyes closed
every night he comes
praying *Allah, Allah*

my body
is dark blue, there are
bones visible
I watch the blue
turn to yellow

day and night
there are bright lights
I know evening
by the voices of my man
my child, the muslim nurse

metal spikes
like blades of grass, grow
from my legs
I lie in an alien field
with poppies and bones

Intensive care unit

the path grows darker

down the path
overgrown with briars
and brambles
we wander chatting
in the late sun

further along
the path grows darker
through tangled woods
we pass old graves
abandoned in long grass

fallen stones
covered in green moss
lie about
the ruins of a shack
hide in thick green ivy

a dank smell
from the water-filled ditches
a coot calls
it's easy to imagine
old deaths and murder here

nettles sting us
crowding the verges
mosquitos bite
nature owns this forsaken place
we are not welcome here

Common Lane, Norwich, England

Joy McCall

they come

cryptids
and lingerlings
haunt me
in dark corners
small eyes shine

among
the garden trees
they move
at night they sing
strange lullabies

I sleep,
and even then
they come
they sing in tongues
sweet, unknown

they smile
their kind faces
downy
their hands gentle
on my own

stay here
brown lingerlings,
take shelter
the ages will pass
my soul is yours

A cryptid is a creature or plant whose existence has been suggested but is not recognized by science. They may be Lingerlings, survivals of species known from the fossil record.

the old wife

For Matsukaze

glad, the old wife
goes now to wash
salad greens
carrying a brown face
in mind, singing

the old wife
reading poetry while
eyesight dims—
trying to fill her memory
with enough words to last

she falls
these troublesome days
over things
songs hanging in the way
and dark people lying

the brown man knows
the right kind of rope
to pull
the old woman
out of her dark pit

the old wife
tires of stirring
endless noodles
and picking supper greens
she takes a long nap

Joy McCall

stones and bones

we are
a pale people
and ancient
going back too far
to remember

our feet
have walked this small place
since the dawn
since the sea fell
and the island came

and man
found solid ground
to stand on
and the great trees grew
and the wolves came

invaded
again and again
we fight back
we tattoo the names
of the vanquished in our skin

we are
a pale inked people
our bones lie
layers upon layers
turning to stone

nephew

For Ben

lunchtime
we speak of lunatics
and the full moon
his quick scorpion
and her heavy-shelled crab

dark
my whiskey coffee
he tells
the names of drumbeats,
tapping the table

I tell him
his gin is juniper
bitter berries
he knew a girl
jennifer juniper

we eat
discussing sex
and tides
the many kinds
with and without hope

the fish
climbing his arm
are darker
the birds take flight
the ocean becomes the sky

The Rushcutters Pub, Norwich, England

monkey gods

the old shrine
abandoned, pillars fallen
vines twisting
a wild deer stands
among the greening

worn steps
slippery in rain
thick with moss
can I climb to pray
or have the gods gone?

nothing stirs
the wind dies down
the rain stops
I am alone
in this silent place

ruined
the stone idols'
broken faces
these are dead gods
without breath

for a moment
a new wind moves
the iron bell
one brief dull sound;
I pray, weeping

Sado Island, Japan

brown man

For Matsukaze

the man
steps out from the pines
into the rain
even drenched, his skin
the colour of the bark

from nowhere
and long ago
he unfolds
from a brown paper page
covered in waka

men like him
they sing the dark blues
on city streets
how did he stumble
into this sterile tea-room?

a pale mind
in a brown body
I wonder . . . .
are the inner eyes
slanted against the sun?

I hear
his long footsteps
on the path
the trees drip water
on brown skin

wild thyme

soft chamomile
quiets the mad hares
in the field—
their brown bodies
covered in pale dust

fennel, wild mint,
and the grey-green sage
wrinkled like bark
or furrowed earth
after the plough

I pick leaves
of wild mountain thyme,
remembering;
when I touch my face
my eyes fill with tears

the wind blows
from the far north hills
and I am lost—
chamomile and sage
cannot calm this longing

rosemary oil
in the jade burner
grows warm—
will it make me remember
what I would rather forget?

The herb garden, Fallow Lane, Norfolk, England

blood spots

I wake
the cabin is cold
it's snowing
the fire is out
the room is dark

a sound
pulls me from sleep
I curl up
pulling the quilts
closer around me

a scent
of wild animal
on the air
rough breathing
outside the door

at the window
I'm shivering
the sky
is thick with stars
the lake is frozen

at dawn
I go to the woodpile
in the snow
a trail of blood spots
I am rabbit, I am wolf

Gold Lake, Canada

napping

For Kate and Wendy

I stood
at the head of the bed
leaning on the wall
my feet moved slowly
beginning to dance

I drove, dancing,
to the great barn
where the artist lived
he was not home
I parked on his lawn

my daughters
came from nowhere, we sat
in the barn
and lit the fire
and drank all the wine

the painter
came home very late
I did not know him
we talked long by a tree
of childhood and books

he did not mind
the empty bottles,
the fire embers
he sang and we all danced
arm in arm, down the long hall

You have to know, I cannot walk or dance or drive a car. My dreams don't know.

pika

in his mouth
yellow wildflowers
and grasses
he makes his bed
deep in the rocks

all summer
he gathers stuff
bunches
he watches the sky
and the shadows

an eagle
passes above him
he freezes
onto the grey stones
silent, one of them

the days grow cold
the flowers die
snow falls
he circles the meadow
one last time

mid-winter
he goes deeper
he eats
the bed he sleeps on
his small body smells of grass

Alberta, Canada

threads

from my bed
in the big hospital
I watch
small spiders
on the window

they weave
wide webs, catching flies
the ward cleaner
wipes the glass
they weave again

I sleep
the doctors come
with needles
and serious faces
and bad news

every day
the spiders spin
the flies are caught
the doctors come
the cleaner wipes

I am caught
held fast in this web
sticky
the invisible dark
malevolent threads

Spinal Unit, Sheffield, UK

the monk and the lady

the woman
is dancing
and singing
purple feathers
in her battered hat

red skirt
swirls wide and high
she laughs
she is a tart
despite the wrinkles

in the doorway
a young man stands
he is solemn
and stays silent
his brown robe is frayed

his long belt
is unravelling
he ties it
contemplating
sad, he turns away

she takes his hand
and draws him in
the cello plays
under the chandelier
they waltz all night

These are parts of my self.

Joy McCall

the house of women

wandering
we reach a strange place
my child and I
the house of women
bids us welcome

in the night
the maniacs come
and steal our bags
they climb over us
and mutter in the hall

they run
up and down the stairs
I hold their hands
and put them to bed
and lie beside them

all night
they pull and pick my hair
laughing
they move the chairs about
and open all the curtains

my child
sleeps in a cupboard
with the door shut
when day comes we will leave
and go somewhere else

watch me bleed

For Barry

I am living
in the half-light
miles below
that thin fearful space
where he spins his days

I say
show me again
where you are
you are fiercely sharp
while I am dull

pull me
out from this shelter
to stand
naked and brave
on the drumming earth

drop
that broken brilliance
like hailstones
for I am tired
of soft comfort

pierce the fog
scatter holes in the dark
let the bright truth fall
let it bite . . .
watch me bleed

the crossing

I cannot tell
what comes next
or how or when
the sands run through
or the mystery unfolds

I see myself
at the crossing
in darkness
in grained oak
and brass and brown velvet

I will not lie straight
in starched white linen
my hands folded
I will curl up bare
against the rough wood

my arms
will make shelter
for those small things
that are too precious
to leave behind

I will hold them
as once I held my newborns
whispering
now these I love,
these matter most

Colney Burial Ground, Norwich

before

from my bed
I watch the morning sky
that pale pink
that follows cold nights
and warm days

before
I would have been up
at dawn
walking in damp fields
gathering flint

the fields
still carry the weight
of those ages
of heavy oceans
before man, before time

today
the knife-edge between
now and then
begins to blur
pain is a shifting mirage

the quilt is silk
I'm holding a small stone
in one hand
a dark weight in the other . . .
I want to walk

dust

in the dark den
the child moves in sleep
a small hand opens
a stone falls on the sand
the wind howls above

the snake
catches its scales
on the stone
and slowly peels
out of last year's skin

the woman spins
in the rape fields
raising dust
her skin grows yellow
and heavy-scented

she shakes her head
it is full of dust
the dust scatters
like bird seed husks
and crumbled leaves

she sleeps
with her child, breathing
the dust of skin
of scales and ashes
and soot and soil

Inner lands

directions

you can
find your way home
in spite of the storm
with the loud thunder
and heavy rain

by the beech tree
that stands alone
turn left
touch the bark as you pass
it is a lonely tree

jump over
the river downstream
the bridge is broken
don't be afraid
of the sudden light'ning

go past the field
where the deer are sleeping
follow the lights
to the low timber house
outside the village

it is not your house
but sleep the night there
the beds are soft
when you wake you will know
exactly why you came

limpets

the island
sighs in sleep
stars appear
small waves break on the sand
the wind breathes across the water

a dark bird
flies down to the meadow
it strides about
picking dandelion seeds
its eyes are quick and black

new-born snakes
slide through the grass
the blades tremble
then settle; the snakes
slip between the rocks

my fingers hurt
the joints, the bones,
from flute-playing
the songs have called the limpets
up to bask in the moonlight

there are bones
lying in the ruins
they are old and brown
I will bury them in the sand
at tonight's low tide

Inner lands

the pied piper

oh rid us
of this plague of rats
the townsfolk begged
and the lone piper came
and began to play

he stood tall and thin
in the marketplace
and his tune
was high and clear
like the song of a wild bird

the rats came
from all their dark corners
and followed him
out of town, along the road
to the drowning sea

the town
rat-free, did not pay
the piper's fee
and so he began again
to play that sly refrain

and the children came
out of all the houses
dancing and singing
and the piper played on . . .
over the hills and far away

This comes from an old nursery rhyme which might have been made
at the time of an early plague in Europe which killed so many children.
The Piper was a symbol of Death, a bit gentler than the Grim Reaper.

violin

washed up
on the bleak shore,
a battered case
the poet walking the cliffs
climbs down

a struggle
to climb back up
he takes care
an old violin, a bow
some wax in a rag

he settles
in the old ruin
and tunes the strings
the air smells of cloves
and seaweed

he plays
a mournful song
to the sea
the wild girl stops dancing
listening, waiting

he plays all night
she sleeps in the long grass
the air is music
the green island hums
speed bonnie boat . . .

Inner lands
The song is 'Over the Sea to Skye.'

falling

I sat
against the pine-tree
by the hedge
watching a dog-fox
running in the far field

hazelnuts
and pinecones
were falling
dropping hitting landing
on the hard ground

a brown bird
began to flap
in the hedge
one wing caught
on a long thorn

the bird fell
close to my hand
how could I not?
I took it and sat still
and quiet, praying

hopeless
the bird was dead
in my hand
I recited *hold fast to dreams**
musky smell of fox on the air

Howe fields, Norfolk

*

Hold fast to dreams
for if dreams die
life is a broken-winged bird
that cannot fly.

Hold fast to dreams
for when dreams go
life is a barren field
frozen with snow.

—Langston Hughes

broken

these fields
are strewn with shells
and flint stones
the bones of birds
of animals and men

I take bits home
small stones, brown thorns
wheat stalks
broken bottles
hard hawthorn berries

on the fire
a thorn is a wish
for a sharp mind
a stalk is a hope
for the thin, the hungry

red berries
burn for the brave
dear ones
cracked bones char
for the heartless few

broken things
bind me to this land
where I was born
I am home, I know
where I belong

Wheatfen, Norfolk

white horse

For Richard

under the pines
the burial ground
and a white horse
standing so still
is it real?

I call
it turns its head
pine cones
crunch under its feet
as it comes

I feed it
dandelion leaves
its eyes are dark
its breath is warm
on my shoulder

my fingers
settle into the mane
and hold on
there is a moment
. . . you know

the horse
watches me as I go
and beside him
a woman with red hair
and wild tattoos, laughs

Iceni marketplace, Upper Stoke, Norfolk

over the hills

For M. Kei

sabbath morning
the meeting house
is quiet
on my horizon
a brief light flickers

he writes
of wings and sails
of sky and sea
my pain falls to the seabed
my sadness lifts and is gone

a low voice
carried on the wind
on the tides
pulls my sorrow
over the hills and far away

he sits
his hands lifted up
to the sky
gathering light
and brings it to me

I go now
to sit on the hill
among the stones
his gift in my hands
to share with the wind

the flute sang

I sleep
under the heavy trees
in the late sun
the sumac seeds
dropping my name

I wept
I want my youth back
the flute sang
a song of rivers
of loss, and passing time

so much
I cannot do, places
I cannot go
I fill the aching spaces
with low flute songs

native flute,
sumac and horn
sing me the wind
sing me the songs
of the deer on distant hills

sing me
the deep longings
the pain
the death of the deer
the birth of the rivers

A Native flute from the Canadian prairies, gift from my daughter.

hollow

in the woods
a small child cries
somewhere near
it is growing dark
I go searching

I find her
in a hollow tree
she is tiny
too small to be in woods
at night, alone

I say
come out with me
but she will not
she says, *I must wait*
for my brown-haired mother

so I sit
close beside her
all night long
the sky fills with stars
the woods fill with noises

towards dawn
she starts singing
and I sleep
when I wake she is gone
and I cry, calling, *oh, child*

Fairhaven Woodlands, Norfolk

wreckage

I tire
of seeing the rowboat
on the rocks
wedged fast there
through the seasons

I watch
the timbers rot
and shift
the sea flows in and out
carrying bits away

I grieve
for the loss of the dream
of journeys
I carry jetsam
up the cliff to the ruin

the wood splinters
in the sun and the wind
I make crosses
to mark the graves
of the old ones

in Autumn
I drag the wreckage
to the shore
and set fire to it
and stare out to sea, weeping

Inner lands

all at sea

I asked
the wild-haired sailor
to change course
to turn toward
the small green island

she said
I am a sailor
all at sea
my home is the wave
the sails, the oars

I begged
pulling at her shawl
and weeping
I cannot abide
this constant rocking

she sighed
if I take you to land
you will stay there
and I will be alone
wherever I go

so I wait
going mad for the sight
of cliffs and hills
in my sleep I taste
nothing but salt

this alien sea

I drift
in deep waters
spinning
in the swelling tide
on the horizon—a boat

raising
a calico sail
the sailor sings
whither thou goest
I will go . . .

salt-crusted
her white hair tangled
she pulls me in
she knows the star-map
we sleep, drifting north

a haze
of silver flying fish
at dawn
the wind dies down
the tide-pull slows

we pass
an island, it is not mine
she sails on
how vast, disorientating
this alien sea

lavender

I sleep
on a lavender pillow
mauve and green
the seeds rustle
when I turn my head

in the wheelchair
I sat in lavender fields
last summer
watching the girls
cutting the stalks

their hands
moved so quickly
and as they cut
they talked of boys
and dancing, and new shoes

they tied
the great bunches
with rough string
and hung them to dry
on high hooks in the barn

when I sleep
I dream of the village hall
and the girls
dancing, spinning, laughing
smelling of lavender

Caley's Mill, Heacham, Norfolk

herring gulls

at the end
of my bed, a woman
in shadow
I hear her breathing
slow and shallow

her fingers
pick at the quilt
scratching
I can't see her eyes
but she is watching me

sleepy
I pinch myself
to stay awake
I do not trust
what the woman might do

she begins
to hum the boat song
a sea shanty
more like a lullaby
I drift to sleep

all night
I dream of waves
and seaspray
and herring gulls screaming
diving, pecking at my eyes

star-song

of course
I should be asleep
but I'm not
I am in the dark
listening to the night-song

stars
are playing violins
the moon
is in hiding
she likes silence

dark clouds
gathering in the north
angry
they don't like the singing
they prefer to shout

the wind
likes to roar and howl
and chase the rain
when the wind blows
I can't hear the stars singing

footsteps
foxes running
up the lane
not barking, quiet
entranced by star-song

goddess

the goddess Freya
the groomer comes
pierced and tattoo'd
her slow Norfolk voice
settles the scaredycat

she's an airhead
mercurial
gemini
she laughs while the tangles
and fur-mats disappear

at twenty
she is covered
in ink
grandma, grandpa on her legs
roses and vines up her arms

her back
is covered with strange
viking runes
she traces her kinfolk
back to the longships

she sees things
spirits of men and beasts
they speak to her
the mad skittish cat curls up
purring at her feet

dark

my poems
are dark these days
I am grounded
like the dark earth
of these peaty fields

black sheep
roam these soft green
Norfolk hills
black crows pick the wool
caught on hedgethorns

a dark
aboriginal face
in my dream
some ancient story
takes human form

a dark rook
in the blackthorn tree
complaining–
I want his voice, his eyes,
his jet-black wings

the hymn
in my blood
flows dark
back to the soil
from whence it came

deal

the devil
showed up again
out of the blue
and offered me a deal
he thought I'd take

one year
he said, *as you were*
before the crash
and then you die
finito, the end

I looked him
in the evil eye
he meant it
he gave me one day
to make up my mind

I thought
of standing, walking
freedom
sex and sleeping
independence

ability
comfort and ease
normality . . .
it took five minutes
to say *yes*

In the church ruin, Thorpe St. Andrew, Norfolk

a penny for the guy

1.

staunch in their faith
the Catholic men
hatch the plot
over cheap ale
in the Dog and Duck tavern

the youngest man
in a filthy airless
undercroft
makes the sign of the cross
blessing the martyrs of his faith

he sweats
hiding gunpowder
under wood and coal
checking his watch
waiting for the signal

English Lords
wigged and robed, in the great hall
above his head
gather in solemn state
passing the laws of the land

heavy footsteps
the priest/betrayer
approaches
the young man is sold
for a few pennies

2.

he is thrown
into the dark jail
mocked and beaten
tortured on the cruel rack
he confesses

tied by his feet
behind the horse
he is dragged
through the streets of London
past jeering crowds

broken
and bloody on the scaffold
still he prays
the god of the Romans
does not deign to save him

his hacked limbs
are scattered north, south
east and west
that he may find no rest
between heaven and hell

centuries later
the children laugh
around the bonfires
Roman candles, sparklers
a penny for the guy

Guy Fawkes Day, November 5th, remembers Guy Fawkes and the Gunpowder Plot, by recusant Roman Catholics, to blow up the Houses of Parliament and kill the new Church of England King.

shrubbery

hiding
in the shrubbery
I watch
the days, the nights
the seasons passing by

moonlight
throws long shadows
strange creatures
wake and wander past
catching my scent

midnight
I follow the course
of stars:
dippers and bears
fish and hunters

at noon
the air is noisy
with bees
I keep silent
other voices are sweeter

the shrubbery
thickens and grows dense
the spiders come
they weave webs in my hair
my bones are pale thin roots

journey

For Barry

it was his idea
to load up with opiates
and travel
over land and sea
to the Himalayas

the drugs
for the certain pain
of the journey
the boat, the train
the mules, the mad climb

I wonder how
he will push the chair
up the mountain
he says *I am Sisyphus*
it is my destiny

then let us
raise the white sails
weigh the anchor
sling the hammocks
and check the wind

travelling
with disabilities
is easy
for poets and dreamers
with unbound souls

root-bound

my dark sister
come out from the roots
of the black tree
it is no place
for a brown woman

come with me
climbing at sunrise
up the green hill
dance for me
until day is done

come, bathe
in the cold salt sea
as the tide ebbs
and dry in the winds
that howl in the dune-grass

at moonrise
the broken bough
for the fire
samphire in the pot
mead in the cup

sleep not
root-bound, my lady
my dark one
the brown holy ground
calls you to bed

Howe fields, Norfolk, England

pit

For the bagmaker

the west wind
blew across the moor
we climbed
until the grey lake
lay far below

the voices
of ancient stones
called to me
I sat in the circle
he went walking

I dozed
his shout woke me
come and see
it was a pit dug deep
by ancient men

a small black horse
lay on its side
long dead
laid out so neatly
its legs straight

remnants
of sacking ties
lay under it
and always now I see it
tied, falling, dying

Barton Fell, Cumbria, England

dominus insularum

sweet Cara
the dear island
calls to me
storm-tossed, wind-swept
across the strand

desolate
she bears the brunt
of wild waves
feral goats, her lovers
under dark skies

I lie there
in my night dreams, curled
in long grass
in the solitary house
fallen to ruin

I listen
to the goats, to the wind
to the waves
and I want him to come back
and hold me through this dark night

Lord of the Isles
do not forsake me
winter is coming
and I hear the pipers playing
the last high song of the sea

Dominus Insularum—Lord of the Isles—the title of the most powerful landowners of old Scotland—the Celtic/Norse Somerled—summer wanderers.

Cara (dear one), a tiny island off the coast of Scotland, is still under the independent rule of a descendant of the great Lords, although no one lives there. It has one ruined house and a herd of feral goats.

blackberries

For Andy

I am
the hawthorn hedgerows
the thickets
and the broken flint stones
caught in the roots

I am leaves
berries, hips and haws
I love rain
it makes gulleys
in my dry skin

a deer
eating bark, startles
when our eyes meet
he turns to run
but stops and looks back

the creature
knows the kindred spirit
of a woman
trapped in briars
held in small stones

the hedge
holds me fast
I learn
how to be dark and sweet
like the blackberries

heather

come then
let us cross the wall
Hadrian built
before they close
these wandering borders

while we can
let us climb mountains
into the mist
let us sleep in the heather
rough as it is

my ancestors
worked here once
at the forge
learning to make the weapons
the claymore, the thin dirk

they fought
in these wild hills
and were banished
do you hear them die,
iron splitting skin?

now the peace
of this high quiet air
whispers
siren-voices calling
from the sweet purple

ripples

the kappa
has gone away to muse
on the riverbed
I bring him eggplant
but he ignores my gift

I go and pick
the best golden squash
for his dinner
still he sulks among the reeds
and will not rise up

even fried noodles
will not tempt him
he hides
deep and muttering
in the green water

I sit
on the riverbank
all evening
frogs croak in the rushes
a kingfisher flashes past

I weep
a small webbed hand
reaches up
touches my toes
and is gone again

The River Green, Thorpe

magpies

For Jordan and Joey

black-eyed
this longtailed magpie
watching me
I weep with pain
one for sorrow

two for mirth
are they mine then
these dark birds?
laughter comes
out of the blue

I sing
half-remembered hymns
from childhood
abide with me
three for a death

four for a birth
a child himself
the new father
curls to sleep
holding his son

five for heaven
six for hell
seven . . .
seven is the story
I will not tell

ruin

it is no use
the house is ruined
beyond repair
there are holes in the thatch
all the windows are broken

the sea winds
howl down the chimney
and rattle the doors
the fire will not stay alight
I am endlessly cold

in the long grass
the sheep bleat all night
wanting shelter
the walls have fallen
in the hill-fold

I should leave
and go to the city
where there is hope
and pleasure and music
and the laughter of children

I pack my bags . . .
the house calls me back
crying through the gaps
if I end my days here
who will ever find me?

Indiana Avenue

For Brian

sitting
on the windowsill
of the high room
I curl up small
waiting for them

the trees are bare
in the park across the road
no one is there
the old brewery
stands dark and empty too

evening
snow begins to fall
big soft flakes
the trees, the grass, the bench
ghostly white now

there are voices
in the room below
quiet, male
I am unheard, unseen
yet I belong here

this is
eternity now
the quiet snowfall
the welcoming floors
the streetlight, the dark stairs

rocking

For Brian

in the corner
a rocking chair
a dark floor
an old cabinet
with many drawers

where
does she begin
rocking
exploring
wondering?

the cabinet
is not hers
to open
there are secrets
hidden inside

she settles
in the chair
waiting
for a long time
in the high gentle gloom

the men sleep
under blue covers
the empty chair
in the corner
rocks slowly, quietly

folding time

For Lynda

kitsune
on the doorstep
singing
folding coloured paper
origami boxes

she hides them
under the front path
flagstones
we walk along over
endless cubes of time

hazelnuts
from the hedgerow fall
on the path
hazel shoots emerge
between the stones

at evening
when we come home
to our door
there is singing underfoot
the whispering of hazel husks

kitsune
when my time runs low
come and dig
and open the boxes
one by one, day by day

*The kitsune (many-tailed fox) of Japanese legend is said to fold time
into small cubes and bury them under sidewalks.*

deliver us from evil

For Sean

carols
from King's College
Cambridge
in the great cathedral
oh holy night

away
in a manger
choir boys sing
to the vaulted ceilings
the gilded lecterns

priests
in royal purple robes
tell the story
from the ancient Bible
and there were shepherds . . .

stained glass
in the high windows
reflects
a thousand white candles
hark the herald angels sing

Jesus said,
blessed are the poor
the humble
those who mourn . . .
blessed are the merciful

Christmas Day, 2013

Joy McCall

que será, será

Christmas eve
on the western shores
the storm hits
a woman's body floats
down a surging ditch

sailors
on the Scottish isles
are landbound
their trawlers smashed
on wave-battered rocks

relentless rain
sweeps across the land
the rivers rise
once again, homes
and belongings are lost

afraid
I lie awake listening
to the storm
with each wild crash, I pray
keep us safe

I do not sleep
through the long loud night
such wasted hours
it is pointless to be fretting
what will be, will be

sailor

For M. Kei

there is a man
who cannot be seduced
by woman
unless she has
white horses in her hair

his heart
is bound by ropes
and pulleys
and weighed down
by a dark anchor

surrender
is not a white flag waving
from the battlements
but a white sail
filling in the wind

he keeps
a distance between ships
and people
the sea he crosses is wild
and fathomless

he hears
the bones of davey jones
knocking deep
the timbers shake
the sailor sleeps

old ink

on the hill
there are ancient graves
pines mark the place
in the overgrown bracken
lean feral cats sleep

rooks gather
dark-winged spirits
pale owls
hunt among the tombs
a ragged dog-fox wanders by

at his gate
the weary old monk
stands watching
how does he survive
nights in this cold place?

alone and ill
in the open hut
snow falling
he writes with the old ink
his small waka songs

oh long-dead monk
on these strange nights
the ties that bind
grow tighter; time slips sideways
into the darkness

The hermit-monk Ryokan, always my sensei.

roadside

the sun
low in the sky
at noon
Yule is not letting go
its bony grip

long furrows
in the bare field
tinged with green
a hare circles
treading his form

on my mind
that Quaker light
oil lamps
and low voices
in a chilly room

yellow gorse
by the roadside
flowering
in mid-winter
long shadows of trees

a crow
sits on a broken fence
calling
I am unsettled
longing for things lost

the far balcony

I seek
my soul, wandering
blindly
down dark corridors
through dusty rooms

I leave
the heavy doors
open
for what if there is no escape
from that last silent room?

my thin
frightened voice
echoes
in the maze of hallways
disturbing the rats

I breathe hard
up the long stairs
and reach
the far balcony
thick with ivy

*wait, my soul
let me not jump
without you
into the blackness
of this empty night*

picture

beyond
a low hedge
a stone shed
in a barren
grazed field

three sheep
in the doorway
huddled
together
in the rain

a bare
windbent tree
a rusted gate
rain puddles
in the furrows

a trickle
in the stream bed
a black rook
hunched
on a broken wall

these
few things
and the sky
as dark as my heart . . .
that was all

made of wood

For Mark and for Bill

he says
step inside
this tree
let your blood be sap
let your skin be bark

would I fear
the falling of leaves
or the woodcutter
or the breaking of boughs
in winter storms?

he says *dance*
in the wildest winds
that bite and bend,
be unharried
in the midsummer sun

he says
there are no obstacles
to the roots:
the soil parts, the stones shift . . .
the coarse cells descend, unhindered

now hazelnuts
fall from my fingers
words
drop like berries on the soil
I am a poem made of wood

queen

what is
this kingless kingdom
whose queen I am?
the borders shift
unsubstantial as ghosts

in the market square
a tiny golden sun
hovers low
the stalls are stacked
with battered old books

the young men
have left to gallivant
in far lands
the rivers run deep red
with the blood of virgins

magicians
wizards and changelings
guard the sacred places
broomstick-mounted hags
circle over the rooftops

tell me
if you know,
what is
this lawless kingdom
whose queen I am?

common

I like
the common people
the man
who walks the lanes
the woman with a patched skirt

let me not
lunch with bishops
and kings
unless they have simple ways
and everyday speech

I like the man
who gathers nettles
for supper
the boy who picks stones
from the hooves of ponies

the girl
with red cheeks
and rough hands
who keeps the fire lit
on chilly nights

and the old ones
who talk in low voices
and give pennies
to the passing kids
over the garden wall . . .

stroke

New Year's Eve
fireworks exploding
the phone rings:
the hospital . . .
my mother . . . a stroke

New Year's Day
weary and sad
at her bedside
machines, IV drip,
gurgling breath

in the chapel
I light a candle
it's quiet
I am alone there
the stable is dark

her bruised hand
won't let go of my own
words come
recognisable
. . . I love you

she smiles
lopsided
she hums
abide with me
the oxygen tubes hiss

blessed be

For the woodman, Tim

holiness
the dark walnut
of wand and tree
the brown stain that seeps
into all my nights

I pass the wand
through the smoke
blessed be
all the beings
that dwell in the dark

blessed be
the sad and the lonely
the lost souls
those who cannot let go
those too far from home

the wood calls
to the bone and fur
roam again
to the scaled ones
share the peat, the sand

take me, black tree
to the place where all things
meet and sleep
blessed be
the sticks, the soil, the stones

moon

the pale moon
a fine sliver
curling
around the dark
earth-shadow

I forget
if it is called new
or old
but it is beautiful
and needle-thin

I see
the night foxes
looking up . . .
what do they think
of the scrap of light?

the birds
don't care about the moon
they roost
under the eaves, I hear them
shifting in the night

the fish know
they rise to the surface
schooling
they want the bright curve
to fall into their dark river

words

For my mother

I walk alone
to infant school
I am three
I am repeating her words
hang your coat on the hook

she is gardening
and I gather the weeds
in a basket
my white pinafore is filthy
she smiles at me

the tortoise
must be buried
for the winter
my mother fills a deep hole
with fresh straw

there is a pig
in the living room
it is hungry
my mother hands me the bottle
and says *feed it*

four years old
on a sandy beach
riding a donkey
my mother leads it
saying *walk slowly beast*

hook

For Rick McClung

his left arm
is gone, in its place
an iron hook
it was long ago
and far away

I see him
in framed pictures
always
painted standing
on some lonely shore

the hook
wrought iron and leather
intrigues me
it is a crude thing
yet beautiful

he was
Odysseus once
ship-wrecked
left with only the hook
and a battered oar

he stands now
on another shore
his tangled hair
the dark hook, tumble
towards me like waves

divide

my mum
so frail today, I left
her bedside
went in the chapel
lit a candle and wept

she says
it's 'Hobson's choice'
life or death
she is content to sit
at the great divide

nurses bring
chocolate pudding
and custard
her favourite
she takes one bite

my man
holds my mother's hand
she smiles
she tells me *I love*
his brown eyes

her head droops
she goes to sleep
we sit
waiting, listening
to her slow breathing

tomorrow

my man
and my old mother
pointing
to heaven
saying goodbye

we made
plans for my seventieth,
mum and I
now it will be my first
birthday without her

I cannot
make sense of how
she crossed
that chasm between
her chair and the white sheets

looking
at her dead face
bemused
she was smiling at me . . .
now where is she?

reliving
her last words
to me
her gentle voice
see you tomorrow

Joy McCall

faith

I feel
my old mother's
weariness
she wants to be done
with her long life

she longs
to be gone from earth
to heaven
she says that God
is waiting for her

she says
I will see my husband
once again
after all these long
lonely years

she will say
husband, this is what
I have been doing
he will say: *well done*
I have missed you

my mother
looks into my eyes
and says
now, my daughter
it is time for me to go

dead

in the hall
hundreds of people
rows of chairs
her funeral service
the last prayer

I go outside
there are street vendors
laughing
showing their wares
selling my mother's shoes

in her room
I look through cupboards
it is chilly
I want something of hers
to keep me warm

I find
a small unhappy creature
on the chair
I wrap it in her sweater
and hold it, rocking

the sun
is shining in my eyes
I wake, puzzled
my dreams know what I deny
my mother is dead

here

there is
the comfort
of things loved
the familiar feel
of wood and yarn

there is
the sound of rain
and wind and songs
and low voices
coming down the lane

there is
the smell of coffee
and candles
the taste of warm sake
and dark cocoa

here I count
the red bead string
by the fire
speaking names, saying spells
watching the trees in the wind

here there are
monks and brown hares
and deer
and sheep and birds
and all the gods, keeping watch

In the holy room

longings

worn steps
into the ground
the hermit's path
where are his bones,
who slept here in the dark?

I curl up
in the heavy blanket
and sleep
the damp chill
wakes me before dawn

a slight sound
I am not alone
in this place
nor am I afraid
of that other

I wait
the air moves
above me
something
brushes past my head

there are
longings everywhere . . .
he tells me
I cannot leave
she begs me to stay

The hermit's cave, Derbyshire

message

reading
an old book*
I am lost
among the trees
where the green man hides

eyes
are watching
in the boughs
underfoot
some small thing runs

I wait
for a message
on the wind
it comes: *close your eyes
go slowly, feel your way*

I stumble
over tree roots
in the dark
a hand steadies me
curling like ivy stems

then I will stay
I speak aloud
my hand shakes
it is midnight
and I see no stars

* *The Chymical Wedding, a novel by Lindsay Clarke.*

view from my bed

birchbark
winter blossom
crabapples
black and white magpies
fading purple thyme

goldfinches
in the evergreen
grey flint stone
moss between the bricks
snowdrop buds

grey rooftops
smoke from chimneys
bare trees
along the railway tracks,
a broken fence

a rocking chair
Japanese scrolls
small candles
the woodman's oak boxes
old temple bells

empty mug
piles of books
banana
chocolate wrapper
sympathy cards

dance

I sit
in the holy room
in denial
the last time I sat here
she was with me

we talked
about the old oar
I found
I bought the boatman
an evening of ale

Odysseus
listens when I speak
of ships lost at sea
and the silent ghosts
of drowned seamen

there are books
on old oak shelves
my mother picks
Langston Hughes
and reads to me

her voice breaks:
slim, dancing Joy . . .
once you were
I take her hand
we pretend to dance

Sami woman

the night wind
tells me I must go far
and find her
the wild nomad
the singer of songs

she carries
a bag made of fishskin
dyed red
and blue . . . I ache
for the dry scales

she beats
a drum of reindeer hide
I weep
let the reindeer run free
on the tundra

she says
these creatures are
my ancient gods
they give me their lifeblood
they die, knowing

the winter wind
across the barren plains
howls louder
she rolls her long red hair
inside the sheepskin hat

The Sami are an ancient indigenous people who still inhabit remote
northern parts of Scandinavia and Russia.

Joy McCall

forgotten bones

a full moon
the first of the year
small and pale
shines on the fresh earth
between the gravestones

the children
lie in their beds weeping
for their mother
the old gravedigger
nods off by the pub fire

the gates are shut
the cemetery is quiet
stars come out
there's a sighing
of forgotten bones

night rains fall
an owl calls her name
from the trees
a stray cat chases mice
among the stones

cold dawn breaks
a hundred snowdrops
push through the soil
on a stone cross
a blackbird is singing

Author's Note

I began to write sets of five tanka a long time ago because I found that while one tanka was fine for a snippet, a truth, an image—to tell stories, I needed more. Five tanka seemed right.

I began to send the sets to journals. M. Kei used the name *pentaptychs* for sets of five tanka.

Often, naming a thing makes it so, gives it substance. I began to write almost entirely in pentaptychs.

I sent so many to Kei for *Atlas Poetica* submissions, that he said *make a book of pentaptychs*. I said *I don't know if I can*. He said *try, and I will edit it.*

So I tried. And now I am caught in the pentaptych hedgerows and not likely to come out again any time soon.

Joy McCall

Many was the time, while reading "hedgerows," that I sat back in my chair and said "Wow." All of the poems in this book are beautiful, many are very moving; a few defy criticism. I believe that Joy McCall's poetic voice is one of the truest and strongest you will ever hear.

—Jonathan Day, artist and maker of books

Joy McCall's voice grows more powerful with her latest collection of tanka, "hedgerows." As with her previous book, ("circling smoke, scattered bones"), "hedgerows" presents tanka of an exceedingly narrative intimacy. Here are poems about the harrowing ordeals of living with disability and its ongoing health crises, poems of deep love and grief often informed by an equally deep ambivalence, poems of profound empathy with landscape and locale, poems of faith, doubt and even the "supernatural."

Refusing false demarcations between any aspect of her life, McCall never consents to separate or address them singly. In the language of Traditional Witchcraft, "riding the hedge'" is an expression for the ecstatic experience of the witch straddling the boundaries between this and the "Otherworld." Doing so, s/he gathers power to affect change in both. For McCall, the hedge she rides takes the form of the pentaptych, a technical form with which she achieves a mastery so unobtrusive, the uninitiated reader might not notice it at all.

"Hedgerows" insists on being a book of excellent poetry first, a book of tanka second. Somehow that feels right if slightly daunting to those of us also writing in the genre. At the very least it is the mark of authentic experience, again bringing to our attention a poet of real stature working at the apex of her art.

—Brian Zimmer, tanka poet

Hedgerows are part of England's heritage, as fundamental to our landscape as Shakespeare is to our literature. In 1882, William Cobbett in his Rural Rides, described hedgerows "full of shepherd's rose, honeysuckle and all sorts of wildflowers"; he spoke of walking field to field, with such blooms one side, corn the other: "pleasure grounds indeed!" Hedgerows are vibrant ecosystems, havens to wildlife, if only we will let them be. Joy McCall understands them . . . and she hears the poetry within.

These ninety-five tanka pentaptychs (short sequences of five tanka) recall the recently reclaimed art of hedge-laying and bring new stems, or 'pleachers', to tanka's ancient roots. Out of the twisted, tangled darkness come women, witches, ghosts, intensive care units, public houses, graveyards, people and places near and far. Joy's is a life of many lives. She dwells in the belly of the deer. The hymn in her blood "flows dark back to the soil from whence it came". She is leaves, berries, hips and haws. Spiders come to weave webs in her hair. She makes deals with the devil.

Look deep and you, too, will be "caught in the pentaptych hedgerows", and like their creator, you'll be unlikely "to come out again anytime soon."

—Claire Everett, Editor of Skylark & Tanka Prose Editor at Haibun Today.

Made in the USA
Columbia, SC
01 December 2021